To my friends I

POLAND
A. KRAUZE 1981

ANDRZEJ KRAUZE'S POLAND

WITH A PREFACE BY

GEORGE MIKES

NINA KARSOV
LONDON 1981

Acknowledgements

I would like to thank my wife Malgosia A. Pióro
and also Richard Adams, A. B., Malgosia Gago and Amabel Marten
for translating my work.

First published in Great Britain in 1981
by **Nina Karsov**
28 Lanacre Avenue, London NW9 5FN

British Library Cataloguing in Publication Data

Krauze, Andrzej
Andrzej Krauze's Poland.
1. Caricatures and cartoons – Poland
2. Poland – Politics and government
– Caricatures and cartoons
I. Title
741.5'9438 NC1670.K/

ISBN 0-907652-01-8

Reproduced from copy supplied,
printed and bound in Great Britain
by Billing and Sons Limited and Kemp Hall Bindery,
Guildford, London, Oxford, Worcester

Among the numerous able English cartoonists there were two outstanding ones – neither of them English, by the way. The first was David Low, a New-Zealander, the other Vicky, a compatriot and friend of mine. Vicky had a Hungarian passport and liked calling himself Hungarian but he was born and bred in Berlin and spoke only a few words of Hungarian (which he liked practising on me). In any case, he came, more or less, from the same brilliant, exciting but, in this country, little known region of Europe as Andrzej Krauze.

I remember one single leading article from the Low–Vicky era: the one in which *The Times* suggested that Czechoslovakia should be carved up (and I do not remember that one with any particular affection). I have forgotten all the others but many Low and Vicky cartoons – depicting the political problems of the day and commenting upon them – are clearly in my mind.

Krauze's drawings have the same clarifying quality. It is not just the quality of flashlight. A flashlight just lights up the darkness for a split second and gives us a true and realistic picture. Good cartoons also can bring home the truth with great effect but they distort it in a paradoxical manner: so that the truth, in a mysterious way, becomes truer. And there is another difference: when that dazzling split-second of the flashlight is over, total darkness reigns again; but once the flashlight of a great cartoon has created a picture in our mind the darkness is never quite so dark as before.

A first-class cartoon always adds a new dimension to the picture. One of Krauze's drawings depicts Poland as a miserable old beggar, holding out his hat to the world. This is a poignant way of describing Poland's plight. Yes, we all know about the country's threatening bankruptcy. But Krauze's drawing goes further; it tells us something about the Poles' hurt pride, too. They resent being the poor man of Europe; it is a shame to sit on the pavement and beg for alms. And the question lurks in the background: why do we have to beg? Who is responsible for it all?

There is a great difference between Vicky's and Krauze's situation. Vicky – while he needed courage too – could say whatever he wanted and was in no danger whatsoever. Krauze was working in a totalitarian country. In a democracy a political joke is just a joke the subject of which happens to be political; in a totalitarian country a political joke can be – and often is – regarded as *lèse majesté*, treachery and a capital offence. Many people were tortured and killed in Hitler's Germany and Stalin's Russia for having told a joke against the dictator or about the regime. Yet, the jokes and jesters were irrepressible. Every joke is a nail in the dictator's coffin; every joke is the cry of a free man.

The situation in Poland is not quite so bleak. But, as Krauze shows us, the helpless sheep is situated between an all-powerful shepherd and a vicious wolf – that is called "geographical situation"; or – a variation on the theme – he cries out: "Long live the friendship between the sheep and the wolf!" Poland has figured a great deal in the world's news lately. Solidarity, the free Trade Union as well as the personality of the Polish Pope kindled people's imagination. About fifteen of Krauze's drawings collected in this anthology have appeared in the Polish press. As long as Poland can produce outstanding leaders like Pope Wojtyła and Lech Wałęsa and excellent artists like Andrzej Krauze and as long as the Polish regime possesses enough sense of humour, or else is wise (or perhaps just weak) enough to tolerate the appearance of these cartoons, everything is not lost and there is hope for the future.

George Mikes

Propaganda sukcesu

A Propaganda of Success

And this is what they call a geographical position!

Да здравствует дружба между волками и овцами!

Помните про волка!

Remember – if it's not me, there's always the wolf!

Никакие это не государственные соображения, просто извращение!

Raison d'état?

Всегда остается возможность, что он подавится!

There’s always a chance he’ll choke!

Granny, Wolf, Little Riding Hood and the Hunter – the need for co-operation

Я, конечно, очень рад, что барсуки досрочно сдали четыре новые норы, но морковки как не было, так и нет!

I'm delighted that the badgers have surpassed their production norms by digging more burrows, but I wouldn't mind the carrot!

Торжественная встреча или Старый Год дружески приветствует Новый

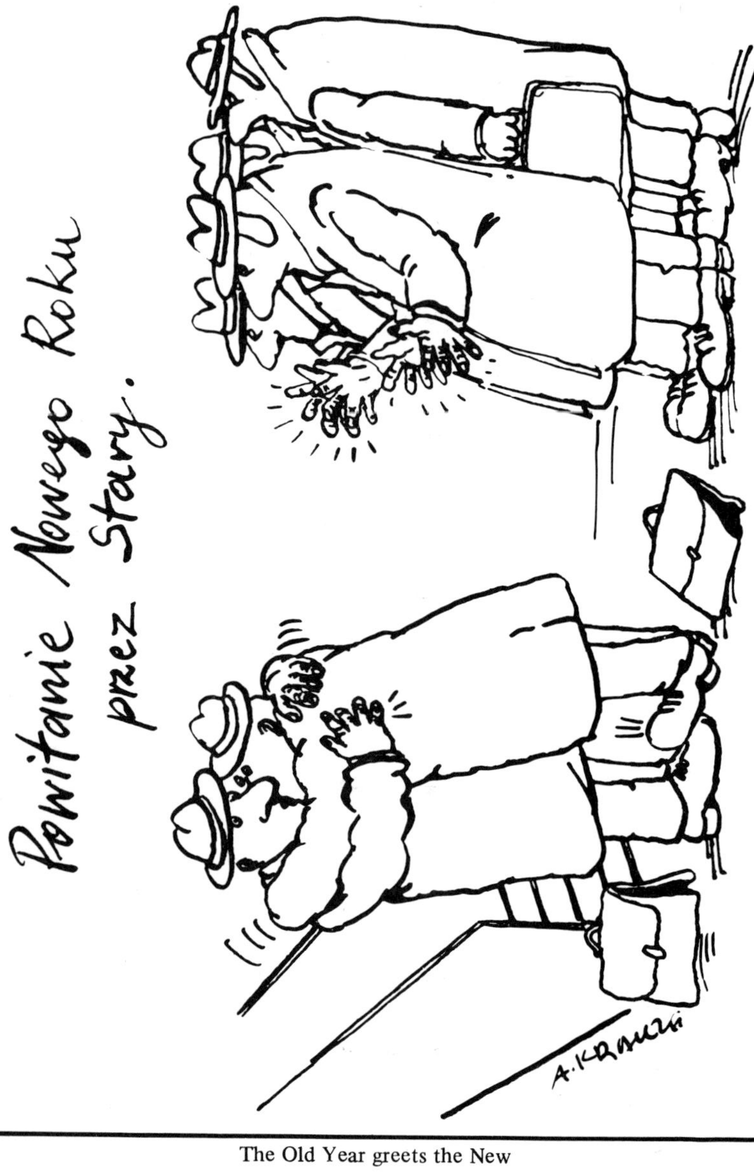

The Old Year greets the New

Разговор с читателями или за более тесные контакты прессы с трудящимися:
– Утю-тю, утю-тюшеньки...

The press getting the message across to its readers

A.KRAUZE/73

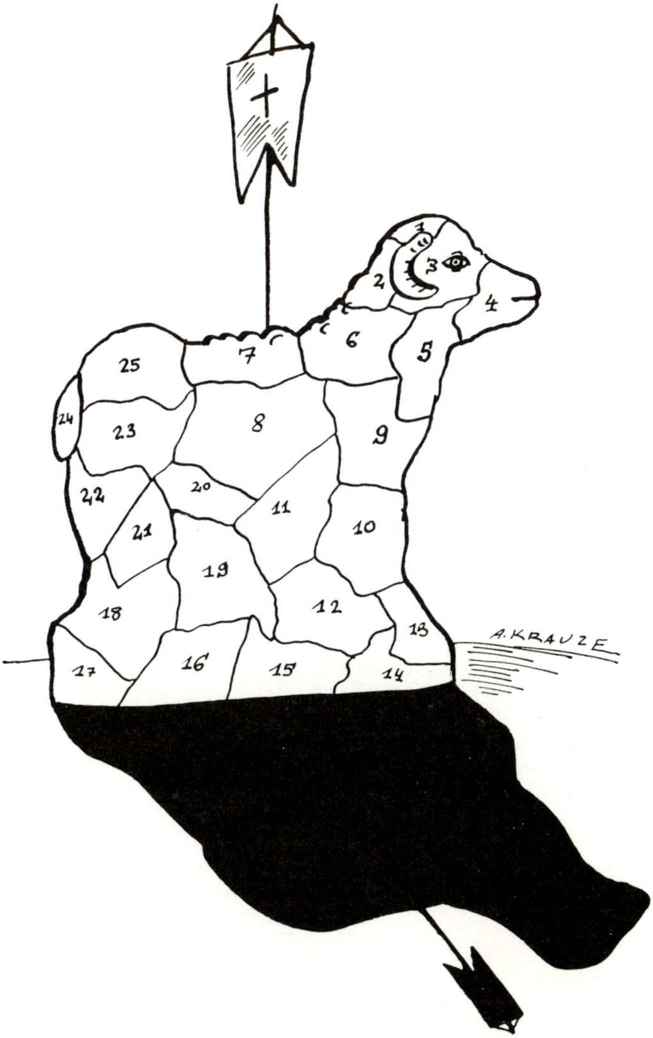
1
2
3
4
5
6
7
8
9
10
11
12
13
14
15
16
17
18
19
20
21
22
23
24
25
A. KRAUZE

Новинка на вашем столе: свежий снег из Советского Союза!

New! Tasty fresh snow from the USSR!

Из серии „Чудеса природы”: Человек-паук восточноевропейский

Spiderman from the East

A.KRAUZE

A.KRAUZE

Присуждаю вам звание кандидата наук „honoris causa”

Have an honorary doctorate!

Нарост на лбу от постоянного битья поклонов закрывает глаза. Что делать?

One of these days I'll bow my brains out!

Охота с критиками

The critics catching the scent

А я не жалуюсь – я лаю только тогда, когда Хозяин позволяет!

... but I'm not complaining! I bark when my master lets me!

Лекция о пользе от госхозов для индивидуального крестьянского хозяйства

On the virtues of collective farming

Выездная комиссия оформляет допуск к полевым работам

Farming by committee

А теперь товарищ Секретарь расскажет об опасностях, подстерегающих вас на свободе!

And now our Secretary will tell you about the perils of freedom!

„МОЛВИЛ АНГЕЛ ПАСТУХАМ...”
Польские колядки

“AND THE ANGEL SAID TO THE SHEPHERDS...”
Polish Christmas Carol

Подписание договора о дружбе и сотрудничестве
между Робинзоном Крузо и Пятницей

Robinson Crusoe and Man Friday sign a friendship treaty

Горько, горько...!

Bride meets groom

Что ты мучаешься – и так и этак я тебя сотру!

You don't have a chance!

Самоцензура: Я буду говорить, но невнятно!

Self-censorship

Начинаем очередное представление из цикла „Звук и свет”!

And now the “Son et lumière”!

Сын мой, когда-нибудь все это будет твое!

One day, my boy, all this will be yours...

Неважно, что корабль тонет – лишь бы руль остался в наших руках!

Who cares if the ship sinks so long as we've got the steering wheel!

Lato 1980
Summer 1980

The Baltic wind

A.KRAUZE

Как оздоровить ситуацию среди овец?
Совещание Волка с Полканом

We must tend to the needs of the flock!

И кто же нас дальше потащит?

Who's going to pull us?

Дорогие польские товарищи! Как это у вас нет выбора?
Или наше руководство, или наши танки!

No choice? But you can choose between directives and tanks!

Посмотрим правде в глаза!

Look truth in the face!

A. KRAUZE '81

Свободные профсоюзы

Free Trade Unions

ТРУДНОЕ ИСКУССТВО СОЧИНЕНИЯ ПИСЕМ

„В связи с плохим состоянием здоровья
прошу освободить меня от занимаемой должности..."

THE GENTLE ART OF LETTER-WRITING

"Due to the poor state of my health
I would be grateful if you would accept my resignation..."

SOLIDARNOŚĆ
A.KRAUZE 1981

Да, я болен, но это еще не повод, чтобы сразу прибегать к помощи ветеринара, да еще без моего ведома!

I may be ill but that’s no reason for calling the vet behind my back!

POLISH POLITBURO
Com. Gierek
A. KRAUZ '80

Товарищ Герек, пришла пора, чтобы вами безотлагательно занялись советские врачи!

Comrade Gierek, time you saw a Soviet doctor!

Столько лет вы играли первую скрипку, что пора вам сыграть на дуде!

Comrade Gierek, first fiddle – last tune!

Как это так получается: решения принимаются индивидуально,
а ответственность мы несем коллективную?

Why must individual decisions become collective responsibilities?

С вами говорит ваш старый лгунишка!

"This is your old friend Mr. Doublethink!"

Contest for the title of first courtesan of journalism

23 миллиарда долларов долга!!! Интересно, сколько же тогда приходится в пересчете на душу...! – Да, и на чью?

"Three billion dollars in debt!!! And how much that is per capita?" – "but who's capita?"

За экономические успехи, которые столько лет подсчитывались в злотых, теперь придется заплатить... в долларах! И кто это утверждал, что злотый – неконвертируемая валюта?

Our economic miracle must now be serviced in dollars.
Who says the zloty is not a convertible currency?

CZECHOSLOVAKIA
EAST GERMANY
POLAND
HUNGARY
1980

А теперь придется тебе подрезать крылышки!

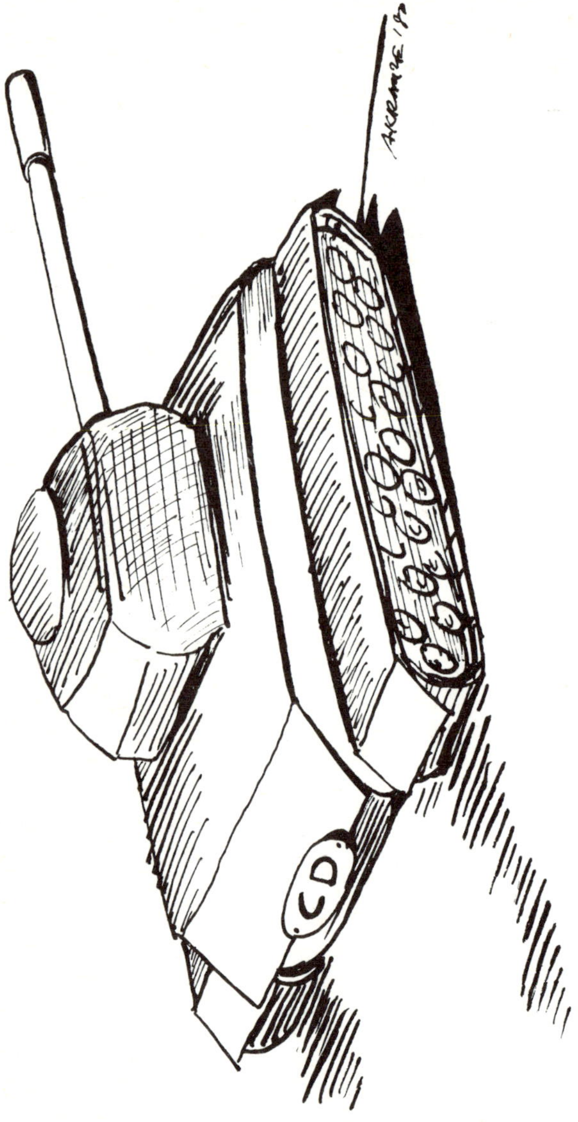
CD

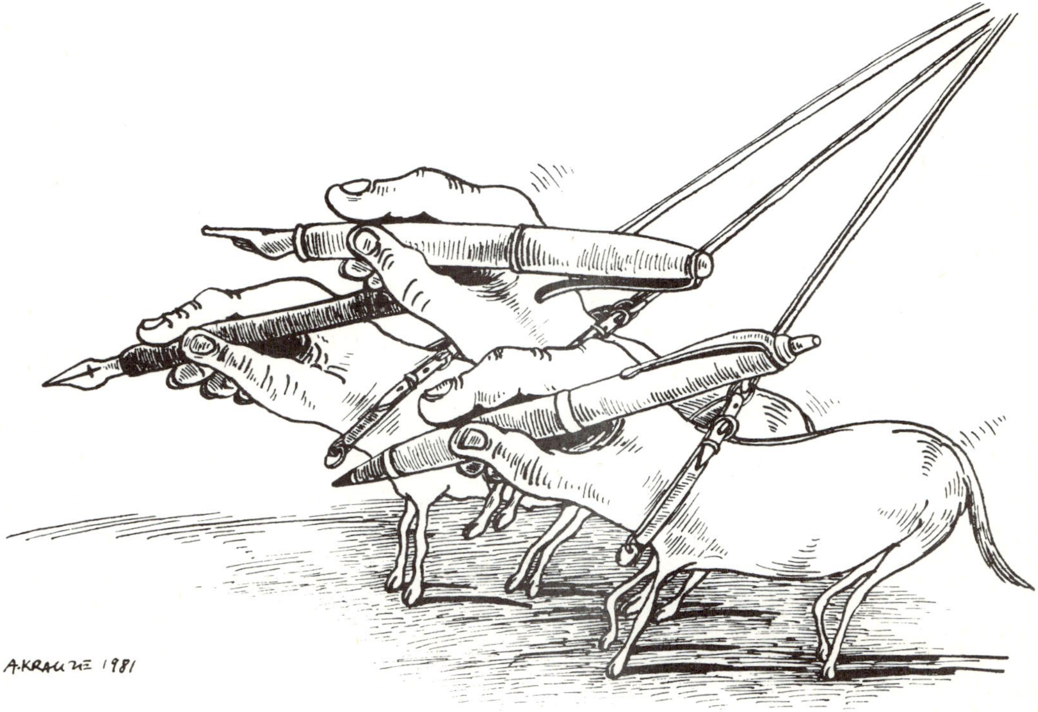
A.KRAUZE 1981

Сдается внаем

Vacant possession

Неброский шарм пролетариата
(на магазине надпись: „Закрыто в связи с отсутствием товара")

The discreet charm of the proletariat. (Closed – no goods)

Мы, бывшие руководители ПНР, действуя в рамках полной демократизации жизни нашей страны, требуем возведения памятника ,,Жертвам Обновления"

We, the former leaders of the Polish People's Republic, also claim our rights accorded under the process of democratization and demand the building of a memorial to the Victims of Renewal!

Если бы рабочие запротестовали на несколько лет раньше, дело не дошло бы до такой катастрофической экономической ситуации. Поэтому непосредственную ответственность за теперешнюю ситуацию в стране несут сами рабочие!

If the working class had risen a few years earlier the economic situation would not now be so catastrophic. It is evident, therefore, that it is the working class itself which is responsible for the present crisis!

Odnowa
Renewal

The end of Simple Simon's rule

Новинки танцевальной музыки: вальс ,,На волнах Обновления”

Everybody’s doing the Renewal Rock!

Да, я отвечаю за весь этот бардак. И что вы мне сделаете?

Well yes, I am responsible for the whole cock-up – and what of it?

~~1956~~
~~1970~~
~~1976~~
1980
1981
POLISH POLITBURO
Reforms
POLISH WORKERS
A. KRAUZE '81

A. KRAUZE 1981

А что касается процесса Обновления, то я отпустил усы!

See my moustache? Not bad, eh? My little contribution to Renewal!

Мы согласны на Обновление – при условии, что нас не тронут!

Yes, we agree to Renewal so long as it doesn't affect us!

О руководящей роли партии

The leading role of the Party

И помните, товарищи: и ,,Солидарности" свечку, и партии огарок!
И нашим и вашим!

Look here, comrades! We've got to hedge our bets in the Party – Solidarity stakes!

ОТВЕТСТВЕННОСТЬ ЗА СЛОВО

– Я пишу так, как мной рука водит! – А я вожу так, как голова велит!
– А я так велю, как мне советуют доброжелатели!

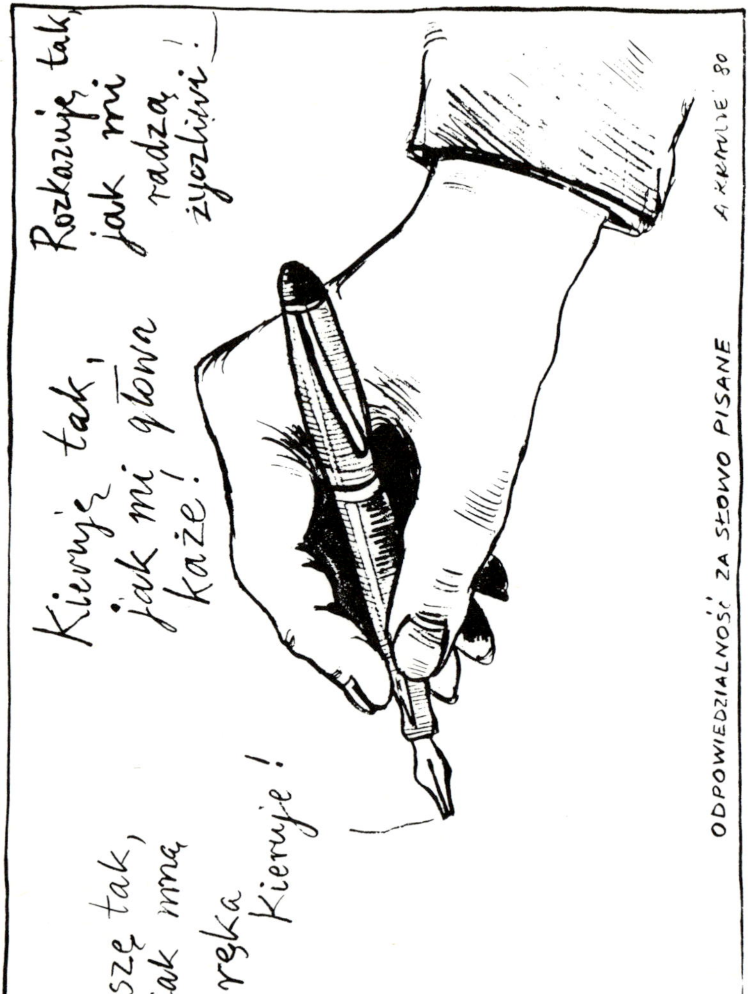

RESPONSIBILITY FOR THE WRITTEN WORD

I write as my hand directs – I direct as my head dictates – I dictate as my brothers desig

Папа, я слышу, как говорят: „Цензура зажимает”. А цензуру зажать нельзя?

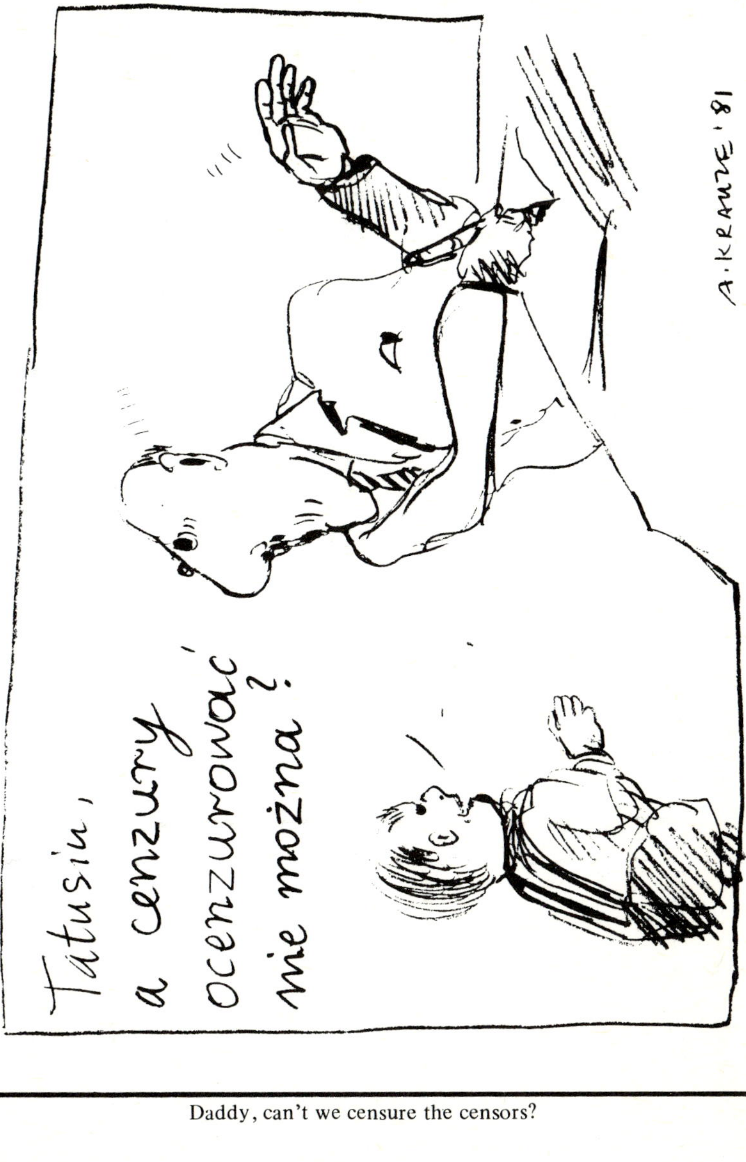

Daddy, can't we censure the censors?

1
2
3
4
5
6
7
8
9
10
11
12
13
14
15
20
A. KRAUZE

Новинка! Диапозитивы с мясом! Большой выбор!

New! A large selection of meat slides!

На полках в магазинах хоть шаром покати, у меня в столе – тоже.
Значит, я смело могу заявить, что мое творчество отражает действительность!

In these times of economic shortages I wish they would ration inspiration!

Сэкономь на Рождестве – сфотографируйся!
Веселого Рождества!

Save on Christmas dinner!

В рамках солидарности с „Солидарностью" мы готовы немедленно отправить в Польшу любое количество танков!

Our solidarity with Solidarity has two caterpillars and a turret!

Как это так получается, что самые острые атаки по нашему адресу
в польской печати не производят на меня ни малейшего впечатления,
а от самой крохотной заметки в „Правде” у меня сразу же сердечный припадок?
– Наверно, у них журналисты лучше!

“I wonder why even the fiercest attack in our press has not the slightest effect on me,
whilst the tamest mention in ‘Pravda’ makes me tremble”.
– “Maybe they’ve got better journalists!”

Папа, он со мной играть не хочет!

Daddy, he doesn't want to play with me!

Доктор, пропишите мне что-нибудь от Солидарности!

Can you give me a vaccination for Solidarity?

Как разделить мясо?

Now, how shall we carve up this joint?

Ну, товарищи, за работу!

O.K. boys, break this horse!

Переговоры о присутствии селедок и карпов за рождественским столом

We'd like to negotiate our presence on your plates at Christmas!

SOLIDARNOŚĆ
A.KRAUZE 1981

Как оздоровить агонизирующую экономику?

How can we cure this economy?

Дорогой, какое счастье, что мы еще не на карточки!

Hallo darling, glad you don't come on a ration card!